GIRLS vs. GUYS

SURPRISING DIFFERENCES BETWEEN THE SEXES

MICHAEL J. ROSEN

TWENTY-FIRST CENTURY BOOKS / MINNEAPOLIS

Twenty-First Century Books
A division of Lerner Publishing Group, Inc.
241 First Avenue North
Minneapolis, MN 55401 USA

For reading levels and more information, look up this title at www.lernerbooks.com.

Main body text set in Avenir LT Std 45 Book 11/15. Typeface provided by Adobe Systems.

Library of Congress Cataloging-in-Publication Data

Rosen, Michael J., 1954–
    Girls vs. guys : surprising differences between the sexes / by Michael J. Rosen.
        pages   cm
    Includes bibliographical references and index.
    ISBN 978–1–4677–1610–9 (lib. bdg. : alk. paper)
    ISBN 978–1–4677–4789–9 (eBook)
    1. Sex differences—Juvenile literature. 2. Gender identity—Juvenile literature.
I. Title.
BF692.2.R67 2015
155.3′3—dc23   2013021833

Manufactured in the United States of America
1 – PC – 7/15/14

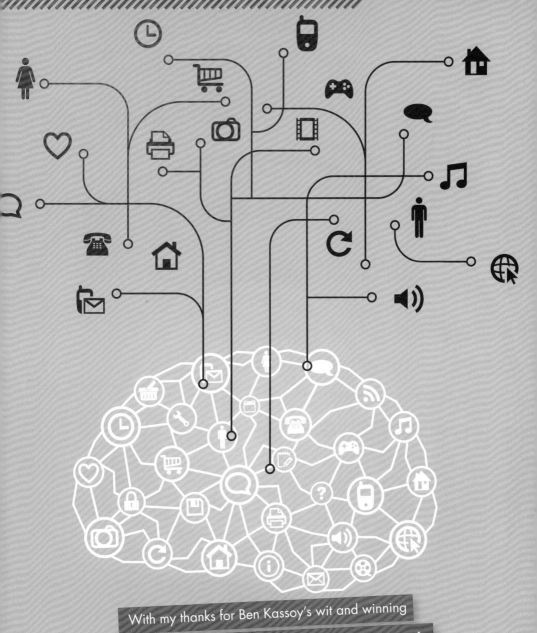

With my thanks for Ben Kassoy's wit and winning collaboration, and the research and drafting efforts of Christoffer Strömstedt, Emily Taylor, and Claire Hamilton

CONTENTS

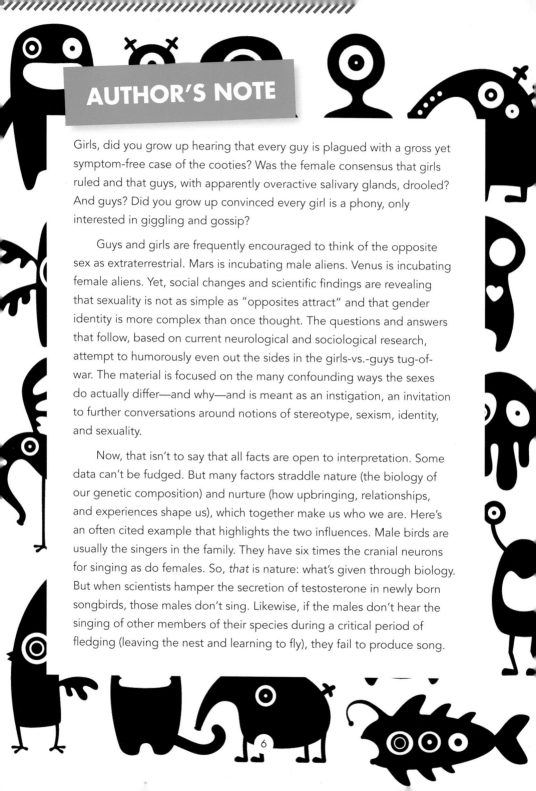

AUTHOR'S NOTE

Girls, did you grow up hearing that every guy is plagued with a gross yet symptom-free case of the cooties? Was the female consensus that girls ruled and that guys, with apparently overactive salivary glands, drooled? And guys? Did you grow up convinced every girl is a phony, only interested in giggling and gossip?

Guys and girls are frequently encouraged to think of the opposite sex as extraterrestrial. Mars is incubating male aliens. Venus is incubating female aliens. Yet, social changes and scientific findings are revealing that sexuality is not as simple as "opposites attract" and that gender identity is more complex than once thought. The questions and answers that follow, based on current neurological and sociological research, attempt to humorously even out the sides in the girls-vs.-guys tug-of-war. The material is focused on the many confounding ways the sexes do actually differ—and why—and is meant as an instigation, an invitation to further conversations around notions of stereotype, sexism, identity, and sexuality.

Now, that isn't to say that all facts are open to interpretation. Some data can't be fudged. But many factors straddle nature (the biology of our genetic composition) and nurture (how upbringing, relationships, and experiences shape us), which together make us who we are. Here's an often cited example that highlights the two influences. Male birds are usually the singers in the family. They have six times the cranial neurons for singing as do females. So, *that* is nature: what's given through biology. But when scientists hamper the secretion of testosterone in newly born songbirds, those males don't sing. Likewise, if the males don't hear the singing of other members of their species during a critical period of fledging (leaving the nest and learning to fly), they fail to produce song.

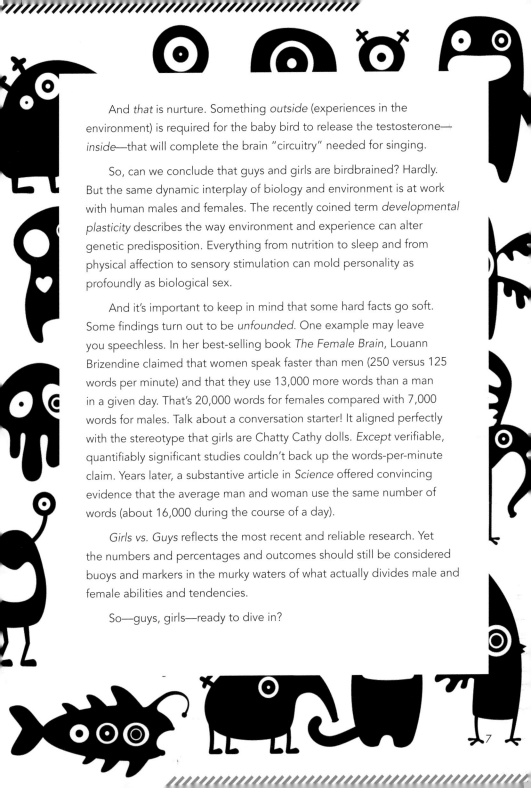

And *that* is nurture. Something *outside* (experiences in the environment) is required for the baby bird to release the testosterone—*inside*—that will complete the brain "circuitry" needed for singing.

So, can we conclude that guys and girls are birdbrained? Hardly. But the same dynamic interplay of biology and environment is at work with human males and females. The recently coined term *developmental plasticity* describes the way environment and experience can alter genetic predisposition. Everything from nutrition to sleep and from physical affection to sensory stimulation can mold personality as profoundly as biological sex.

And it's important to keep in mind that some hard facts go soft. Some findings turn out to be *unfounded*. One example may leave you speechless. In her best-selling book *The Female Brain*, Louann Brizendine claimed that women speak faster than men (250 versus 125 words per minute) and that they use 13,000 more words than a man in a given day. That's 20,000 words for females compared with 7,000 words for males. Talk about a conversation starter! It aligned perfectly with the stereotype that girls are Chatty Cathy dolls. *Except* verifiable, quantifiably significant studies couldn't back up the words-per-minute claim. Years later, a substantive article in *Science* offered convincing evidence that the average man and woman use the same number of words (about 16,000 during the course of a day).

Girls vs. Guys reflects the most recent and reliable research. Yet the numbers and percentages and outcomes should still be considered buoys and markers in the murky waters of what actually divides male and female abilities and tendencies.

So—guys, girls—ready to dive in?

1 A STRIKING DIFFERENCE

It's thundering. Your dog is panting, pacing, and fretting. Your mother is worried and anxious. Your father hasn't noticed a thing. In terms of actually being struck by lightning, who should be more frightened in a storm, guys or girls?

Years of data prove—*inarguably*—that boys should be much more afraid of a lightning strike than girls. The problem is, they aren't.

In the United States, from 1995 to 2008, 648 people were killed by lightning. Of these, 551 were male. That's 85 percent! Efforts have been made to uncover a biological cause for this overwhelming statistic, but no prominent cause has been found.

According to an official at the National Weather Service, guys simply take more risks in lightning storms. They are less likely to stop their activities because of bad weather. When it comes to fishing, camping, and golfing, a guy's plans aren't going to be interrupted by a little heavenly electricity!

So, can the higher fatality rate be explained by males just being oblivious? Maybe not. Part of the explanation might also come from the fact that boys are more likely to be involved in outdoor jobs and activities. Fishing and golfing, for example, are male-dominated activities, and these recreational sports are involved in about half of all lightning-related deaths.

Wondering what your chances are of being struck by lightning? Based on a US population of 310 million and the average number of deaths and injuries from lightning strikes from 2000 to 2010, the National Weather Service predicts that the risk—whether you're a guy or a girl—is 1 in 775,000. Live to be eighty, your chances increase to 1 in 10,000.

Whatever the logic, guys, what's irrefutable is that in stormy situations, do not defy Mother Nature. Go with your feminine side: get inside.

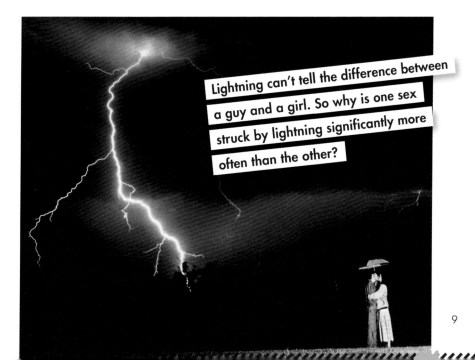

Lightning can't tell the difference between a guy and a girl. So why is one sex struck by lightning significantly more often than the other?

2 SOME LIKE IT HOT

When it comes to a particular activity, girls perform better than guys if the room is about 6°F (3.3°C) hotter. What is it they're doing?

Learning.

And speaking of learning, what recently surprised scientists? Studies show that the hippocampus, the brain region responsible for memory, is larger in females. No wonder a girl remembers exactly what a guy said three weeks ago that doesn't sync with what he just said he said.

Some studies show that females also tend to have a larger corpus callosum, a region of neural fibers that connects the brain's two hemispheres and facilitates communication between them. Therefore, girls are masters of multitasking—doing squats while checking Facebook on the cell phone and talking on speakerphone and lint-rolling cat hair from their pants. Guys are better suited to compartmentalizing and focusing on specific tasks such as ignoring text messages from their parents while playing FIFA as if it were a World Cup playoff game.

But what's the real reason guys might be distracted in the heat of the moment? Research shows that a male's shorter attention span could be attributed to temperature. Boys simply don't learn as well when it's warmer. So, when guys joke that they're "too hot to handle," they may actually be too hot. At least, too hot to perform well and focus . . . without fidgeting or falling asleep.

Girls learn best at a room temperature of 75°F (23.9°C). Guys do better at a cooler 69°F (20.5°C).

Therefore, girls, if you really want to teach your guy something, get him chillin' first.

Room temperature directly affects learning ability. Turn up the heat, and one sex performs better. Turn it down, and the other sex does.

3 NOT-SO-WHITE LIES

Researchers studying the Five-Second Rule for eating food dropped on the floor found that 25 percent of the guys—but only 14 percent of the girls—are guilty of something. What?

They're guilty of fibbing by saying they've cleaned something they actually haven't cleaned.

Sure, we all tell white lies once in a while. You don't have your membership card—not because it's in your "other" gym bag but because you lost it. You're late—not because of an accident that backed up the freeway but because you overslept. We invent white lies to save ourselves or others from overwhelming truths or painful information. However, a recent study points out that people also use white lies to avoid embarrassment and to make themselves look better. This same study tells us that in an average year, guys cook up about two or three lies each day for a yearly total of 1,092. Not only do guys lie more, but they fib about different things than girls.

What are the most frequent lies on a dude's list? Excuses for being late or missing a phone call.

Pretending they were home earlier or had less to drink than the facts show. So, are girls honest angels? A typical female tosses out a couple of lies a day, accumulating 728 in a year. Roughly 20 percent of girls lie about their weight. Another 26 percent lie about what they spent on clothing. And girls specialize in white lies that boost or flatter another person.

So, in the end, both sexes are fibbers. The desire to be seen in the best light possible is simply human nature. Do we lie to seem like a better person? Sounds like a contradiction.

Yeah, well, the truth is complicated.

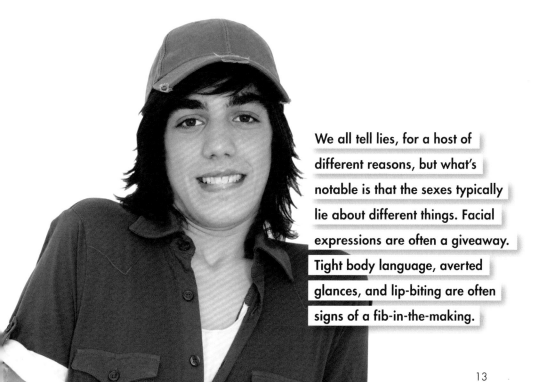

We all tell lies, for a host of different reasons, but what's notable is that the sexes typically lie about different things. Facial expressions are often a giveaway. Tight body language, averted glances, and lip-biting are often signs of a fib-in-the-making.

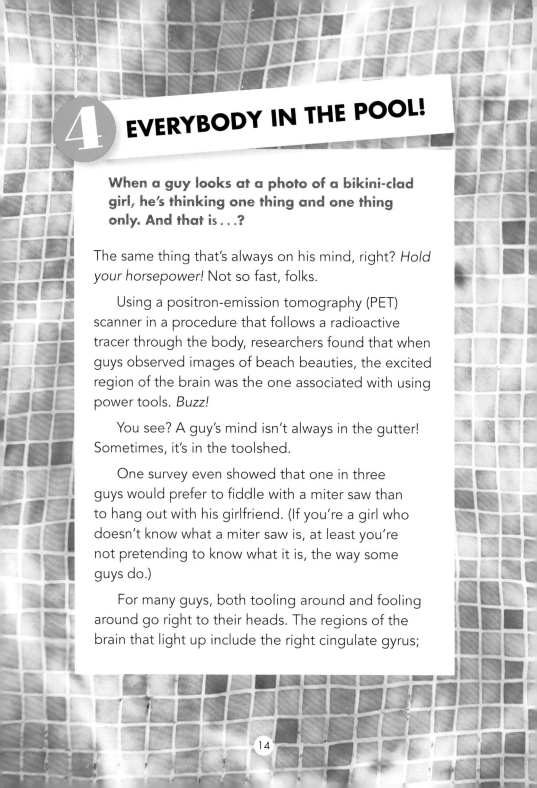

4 EVERYBODY IN THE POOL!

When a guy looks at a photo of a bikini-clad girl, he's thinking one thing and one thing only. And that is . . .?

The same thing that's always on his mind, right? *Hold your horsepower!* Not so fast, folks.

Using a positron-emission tomography (PET) scanner in a procedure that follows a radioactive tracer through the body, researchers found that when guys observed images of beach beauties, the excited region of the brain was the one associated with using power tools. *Buzz!*

You see? A guy's mind isn't always in the gutter! Sometimes, it's in the toolshed.

One survey even showed that one in three guys would prefer to fiddle with a miter saw than to hang out with his girlfriend. (If you're a girl who doesn't know what a miter saw is, at least you're not pretending to know what it is, the way some guys do.)

For many guys, both tooling around and fooling around go right to their heads. The regions of the brain that light up include the right cingulate gyrus;

the right frontal, occipital, and parietal lobes; both temporal lobes; the putamen; and the olfactory grooves.

Studies show that girls are more aroused by an enticing mood and story line than by suggestive images of bodies. All this lights up slightly different regions of a girl's brain: the right temporal and occipital lobes, the right superior and inferior frontal lobe, the right cingulate gyrus, both parietal lobes, the caudate nucleus, and the right olfactory groove.

Isn't anatomy fascinating?

Girls on the beach and tools on the workbench go right to a guy's head—the same region, in fact.

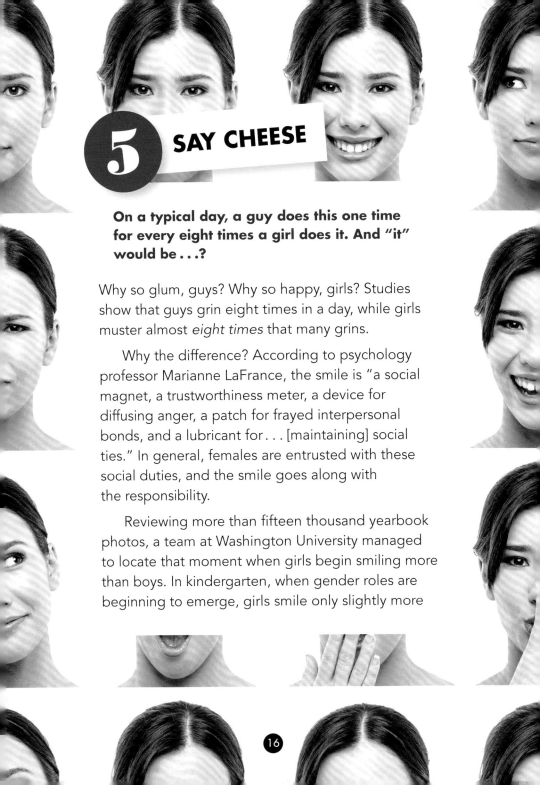

5 SAY CHEESE

On a typical day, a guy does this one time for every eight times a girl does it. And "it" would be . . .?

Why so glum, guys? Why so happy, girls? Studies show that guys grin eight times in a day, while girls muster almost *eight times* that many grins.

Why the difference? According to psychology professor Marianne LaFrance, the smile is "a social magnet, a trustworthiness meter, a device for diffusing anger, a patch for frayed interpersonal bonds, and a lubricant for . . . [maintaining] social ties." In general, females are entrusted with these social duties, and the smile goes along with the responsibility.

Reviewing more than fifteen thousand yearbook photos, a team at Washington University managed to locate that moment when girls begin smiling more than boys. In kindergarten, when gender roles are beginning to emerge, girls smile only slightly more than boys: 59 percent (girls) and 54 percent (boys). But by fourth grade, according to David K. Dodd, PhD, the study's lead author, girls smile more, and "this gender difference widens considerably . . . [by] high school." Looking at senior-class photos, the researchers found that 84 percent of the girls, compared to 65 percent of the boys, are grinning. College photos bear similar percentages. Dodd concluded, "It is surely not coincidental that this period corresponds to puberty and heightened interest in the opposite sex."

So, what's up? What are teens picking up on? The most convincing studies suggest the media's cultural messages about sex roles and typecasting notions of gender help explain why girls smile more. Teens see "stereotypical portrayals of serious, unsmiling men and lighthearted, smiling women," says Dodd. They learn these social behaviors are desirable, so as teens, they begin to emulate them according to gender expectations.

Hmmm, is that something to smile about?

Smiling diffuses aggression, reinforces bonds, and signals attraction. It's a survival skill that's employed differently by males and females.

6 GENDER THROW DOWN

There's only one motor skill in which girls fall far short of boys, performing, on average, only 39 percent as well. And that would be?

World over, when it comes to throwing overhand, guys rock.

In elementary school, girls throw 51 to 78 percent the velocity and 51 to 69 percent the distance boys manage. By high school, the disparity increases. Girls' pitches sail 75 feet (23 meters) compared to 192 feet (59 m) for guys. That's down to 39 percent as far as boys throw. According to Professor Jerry Thomas, a dean at the College of North Texas whose research is credited with first documenting this distinction, "Nearly every boy by age 15 throws better than the best girl."

Nearly everyone who studies gender differences points to this "throwing gap" as one of the few—if not the *only*—verifiable, unbiased, physiological differences. Yet, in "The Gender Similarities Hypothesis," Janet Hyde, professor of psychology and women's studies at the University of Wisconsin at Madison, writes, "The more we argue for gender differences, the more we feed people's stereotypes.

A belief in large gender differences is incompatible with equal opportunity."

So, what is needed for maximum distance and velocity, and why can't a woman's body provide it? Sports science points out that throwing speed builds through the motion of the whole body. Ready to throw, a guy steps forward with one foot, reaches back with his opposite arm, and then rotates his hip and then his shoulder forward. The front of his body opened, he fires the arm forward, the shoulders spring back around, and the lower- and upper-body momentum powers the ball's release. Women naturally turn their hips and shoulders together. Even those women who deliberately practice pivoting shoulders and hips separately can't release the ball with the same velocity as males.

But even Professor Thomas questions whether there's something more than just the fact that guys are typically built bigger and stronger, and with wider shoulders. "I'd bet my bottom dollar there's something neurological. It's the nervous system."

The science of the sexes just isn't rock solid.

> Throwing overhand is one well-documented difference between the sexes. World over, girls move their hips and shoulders in tandem when firing the ball. Boys move their hips first, then their shoulders, leading to a faster, more powerful throw.

7 FLOWER POWER

Let's say you and nine friends placed headphones around pots in which you'd planted tomato seedlings. (So it was a rainy day, and you were bored.) You read them bedtime stories for a month. What would you expect to happen other than having your *other* friends think you're nuts?

Can the voices of human beings charm the natural world? Does a girl's voice affect a plant differently than a boy's voice? Why pose the question unless the answer is yes, right? Right.

An experiment by members of the Royal Horticultural Society of the United Kingdom has shown that in a single month, a tomato plant exposed to a female voice will grow up to 2 inches (5 centimeters) taller than if it were "listening" to a male voice. In fact, some male voices appeared to *stunt* plant growth. Even plants that went to bed *without* a bedtime story grew taller than some guys' tomatoes.

The research horticulturalists running the experiment concluded that human voices, transmitted through the flower pot, acted similarly to other environmental influences on growth, such as temperature, rain, and light. The frequency of the sound waves of an individual's voice influences plant development. A girl's shorter vocal cords create faster vibrations and higher pitches than do a guy's longer vocal cords. And plants appear to respond more positively to the girls' voices.

The voice of Sarah Darwin coaxed the most plant growth of the study. Coincidentally, she is the great-great-granddaughter of English naturalist Charles Darwin, known for developing the theory of evolution. "I'm not sure if it's my dulcet [sweet] tones or the text that I read from *On the Origin of Species* [Charles Darwin's famous 1859 book, in which he laid out his theory] that made the plant sit up and listen," she commented.

Music is a powerful force. Mere sound waves can soothe, excite, inspire, or sadden our human hearts. But did you know plants respond to sound waves too?

8 DRIVE, BABY, DRIVE!

There's one particular way in which an eighteen-year-old guy is similar to his eighty-year-old grandmother. What would that be?

According to the Insurance Institute for Highway Safety, both grandma and grandson are at the same risk for causing an auto accident.

Senior citizens get into wrecks because of vision loss, slower reaction time, health problems, and accidentally drifting into the other lane while distracted. But the senior in high school? His wrecks arise from taking risks. And guys do take more risks than girls do. (That's why car insurance for guys costs so much more!)

Guys are more inclined to disregard the speed limit, to forget to buckle their seat belts, and to forget how many drinks they've had before leaving a party. Twice as often, they turn around to chat with people in the backseat or to talk to people outside the car. And, guys rate their abilities behind the wheel far higher than girls rate their own skills.

What makes girls cause accidents? They're overcautious. This leads to fender benders, failures to yield, parking mishaps, and the unannounced changing of lanes. And, girls are twice as likely to be distracted as a result of texting or talking on a device. They're 50 percent more likely than boys to be groping to get something out of a purse in the backseat. They're 25 percent more likely to be slurping a beverage or biting into an overstuffed burrito while driving.

And if we're talking fatal crashes, guys—for all the reasons above—are almost three times as likely as women to end up in a fatal crash. But if we're talking all car accidents, girls are 12 percent more likely to wreck.

In conclusion, what drives the trouble? The girls' timidity and the guys' temerity.

Insurance is all about risky business. And so are guys. That's why teen boys are charged more for car insurance than teen girls.

9 HEARTBREAK HOTEL

Breaking up is hard to do—yeah, yeah, yeah. But for which sex is it harder?

Even if girls are thought to be more emotional, it's guys who hang out in the lobby of the Heartbreak Hotel after a romantic breakup.

How come guys take longer to recover? The likely explanation has to do with another difference between the sexes. A girl tends to surround herself with confidants, while a guy is close to—oh, *right*—the girlfriend who just dumped him!

Typically, guys keep their feelings to themselves. Yes, research reveals that guys form bonds around activities, in larger groups of acquaintanceships. Girls, on the other hand, establish bonds around emotions and conversation. They share feelings among small groups of intimate friends. So, when life throws a romantic relationship a lemon, a girl gets together with her BFFs to bake lemon bars. A guy just feels sour.

What if the breakup happens to be the result of someone cheating? Who is more likely to seek revenge? It's girls. And what's the most common act of revenge? You'd better watch your wheels, mister. And the preferred target for revenge? Cue the sound of a key scraping a fender.

Let's just say, don't let your car out of your sight.

Guys may try to show a tough face, but a relationship that goes south takes a greater toll on their emotions than it does on girls' emotions.

10 LET'S HAVE A CONTEST!

In which of these four undertakings is a guy likely to outperform a girl? Arranging a date. Winning an argument. Making the bed. Diapering a baby.

You got it. Diapering.

Gaviscon manufactures a heartburn medicine that claims to work in three minutes. In 2010 the company engaged MindLab International to conduct experiments with twelve hundred adults to see what else can be accomplished in the time it takes for the medicine to soothe the belly. Individually, guys and girls tackled a host of tasks in three-minute competitions.

The outcome of some tasks will probably offer little surprise. Change a flat tire? Rewire a plug? Guys won.

Thread six needles? Iron two shirts? Persuade a cop *not* to issue you a ticket? Girls dominated those three minutes.

In four additional tasks—arranging dates, winning an argument, making beds, and diapering—girls outperformed guys at the first three. Yes, that's right. Guys are better at swaddling a baby's bum.

So, what do the tasks guys complete more quickly have in common? They all involve spatial awareness: reading a map, following do-it-yourself instructions, putting up a tent. (You can imagine a diaper is like a little pup tent.) They excel at things that can be done quickly and with less precision.

Women excel when the requirement is speedy hand-eye coordination (threading needles) or verbal reasoning skills (winning arguments, persuading cops). They excel when they can train their entire attention on a single job.

The experiments showed that guys work quickly (they want to be *through* with it!) while girls work diligently (they want to be *thorough*).

The upshot? The world needs teamwork, people!

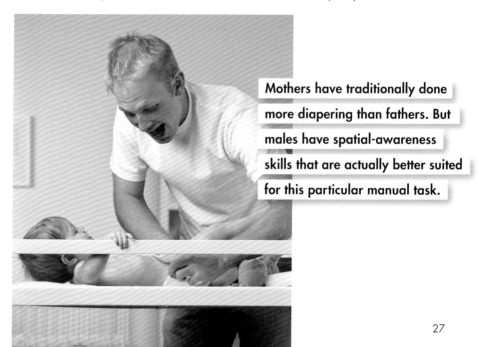

Mothers have traditionally done more diapering than fathers. But males have spatial-awareness skills that are actually better suited for this particular manual task.

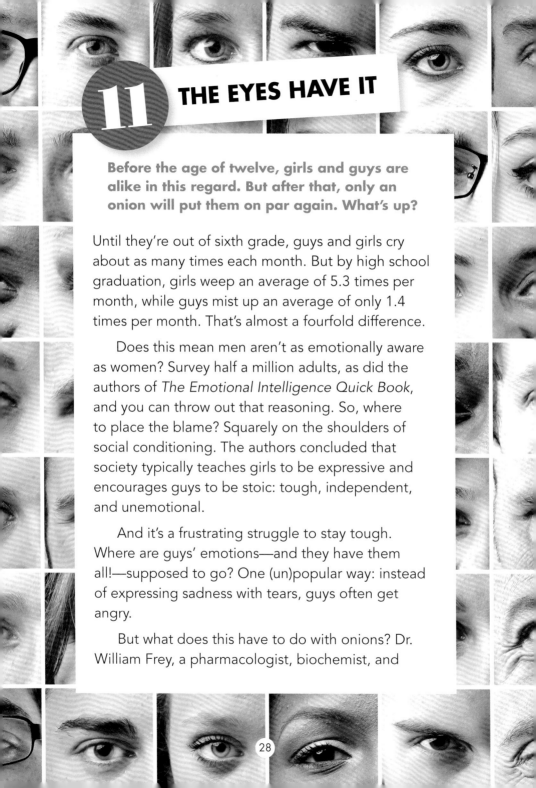

11 THE EYES HAVE IT

Before the age of twelve, girls and guys are alike in this regard. But after that, only an onion will put them on par again. What's up?

Until they're out of sixth grade, guys and girls cry about as many times each month. But by high school graduation, girls weep an average of 5.3 times per month, while guys mist up an average of only 1.4 times per month. That's almost a fourfold difference.

Does this mean men aren't as emotionally aware as women? Survey half a million adults, as did the authors of *The Emotional Intelligence Quick Book*, and you can throw out that reasoning. So, where to place the blame? Squarely on the shoulders of social conditioning. The authors concluded that society typically teaches girls to be expressive and encourages guys to be stoic: tough, independent, and unemotional.

And it's a frustrating struggle to stay tough. Where are guys' emotions—and they have them all!—supposed to go? One (un)popular way: instead of expressing sadness with tears, guys often get angry.

But what does this have to do with onions? Dr. William Frey, a pharmacologist, biochemist, and

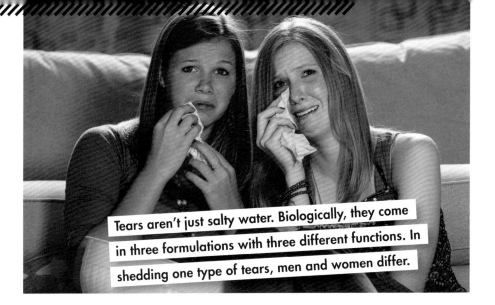

Tears aren't just salty water. Biologically, they come in three formulations with three different functions. In shedding one type of tears, men and women differ.

big cry baby—er, big cry-baby expert—is the author of *Crying: The Mystery of Tears*. He writes that the tears that are shed when the body is under stress—that is, emotional stress—contain hormones. Emotional tears contain adrenocorticotropic hormone (ACTH), which helps the body deal with biological stress. And they have leucine-enkephalin, a chemical messenger that can reduce pain and increase a sense of well-being. And girls shed those sorts of tears almost four times more often than guys.

Both sexes also shed 5 to 6 ounces (148 to 177 milliliters) of basal tears each day; these continually lubricate the eyes. Likewise, there's no difference between guys and girls when the eyes are under the siege of irritants—onion fumes, harsh chemicals, or foreign particles. Then we all shed reflex tears, an irrigating fluid that windshield-wipes the eyes.

Chopping onions or simply blinking, we all cry and cry alike. But for hurt feelings or sappy movies, guys just don't like to go with the flow.

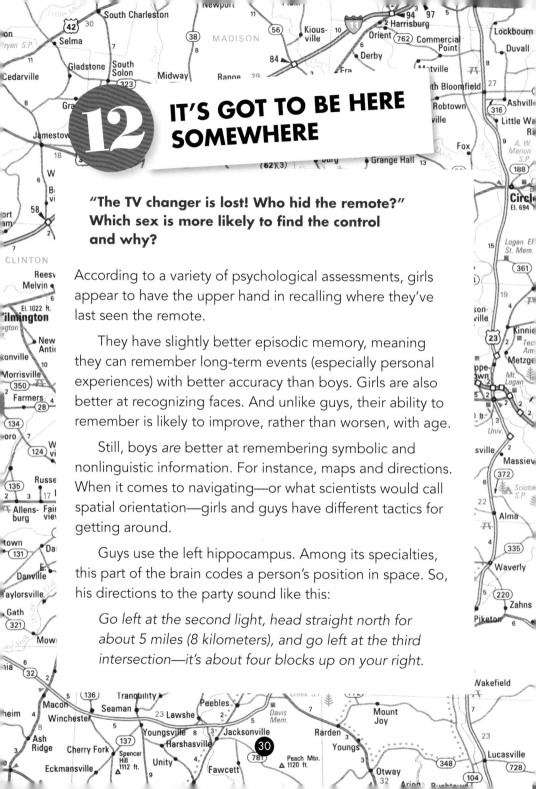

12

IT'S GOT TO BE HERE SOMEWHERE

"The TV changer is lost! Who hid the remote?" Which sex is more likely to find the control and why?

According to a variety of psychological assessments, girls appear to have the upper hand in recalling where they've last seen the remote.

They have slightly better episodic memory, meaning they can remember long-term events (especially personal experiences) with better accuracy than boys. Girls are also better at recognizing faces. And unlike guys, their ability to remember is likely to improve, rather than worsen, with age.

Still, boys *are* better at remembering symbolic and nonlinguistic information. For instance, maps and directions. When it comes to navigating—or what scientists would call spatial orientation—girls and guys have different tactics for getting around.

Guys use the left hippocampus. Among its specialties, this part of the brain codes a person's position in space. So, his directions to the party sound like this:

Go left at the second light, head straight north for about 5 miles (8 kilometers), and go left at the third intersection—it's about four blocks up on your right.

Women engage their cerebral cortex, which focuses on landmarks. So, her directions to the same party sound like this:

Drive until you see the Kiddie Corral Preschool. Turn left and keep going . . . you'll pass the shopping center and the yoga studio, then turn left. Look for the narrow green house with blue doors.

Guys like vectors. Girls like visuals.

Curiously, guys drive 276 extra miles (444 km) each year because they think they know where they're going . . . and won't ask for directions. A British study revealed that one out of four lost guys keeps driving for at least thirty minutes before seeking help. And one in eight guys just keeps driving, never stopping to ask.

Not that girls *don't* drive extra miles too. They tally about 256 extra miles (412 km) each year—missing special landmarks, confusing landmarks, and forgetting turns—to reach a destination.

So, to remember who is having the party, how to get there, and what the birthday kid looks like, the two sexes work well together.

> **The differences in the regions, density, and size of male and female brains means, among many other things, that each sex is better at remembering different types of information.**

13 WHAT'S SO FUNNY?

Girls usually take longer to get there, but once they do, they enjoy it more. So, timing isn't everything. But what is "it"?

All jokes aside, the answer is jokes.

No joke. Girls tend to take longer to get the punch line of a joke. But because they expect less of jokes than males do, girls derive more pleasure from jokes they do find funny.

Researchers have shown that both sexes value a date with a sense of humor. But researchers also found that what girls mean by a sense of humor is someone who makes them laugh. For guys, a sense of humor means someone who laughs at their jokes.

Evolutionary psychologists believe women—the gender that produces and rears the next generation—are attracted to funny men because humor signals intellect and strong genes. These are desirable qualities to pass on to offspring, so females look for potential mates who are funny.

Meanwhile, guys believe girls think they're funny because they are. And that, alone, makes girls laugh.

Humor is a valuable coping strategy. Laughing and a sense of humor rank high on the list of what males and females look for in a mate. Yet the sexes have slightly different reactions to and ideas about laughing matters.

14 BUZZ OFF!

If you were a hungry mosquito, which person would you prefer to bite:

(a) the dude dismissed from the football field for clocking an opposing team member,

(b) a pregnant woman in the stadium,

(c) an overweight kid buying a hot dog,

or

(d) a skinny, out-of-breath cheerleader?

Actually, each of those factors—being male, pregnant, overweight, or out of breath—attract skeeters, which are drawn to scent.

All four of the above-mentioned individuals exude more scent than someone who is female, not pregnant, underweight, and breathing normally. Even from as far away as 98 feet (30 m), mosquitoes can zoom in on our odoriferous skin.

As reported in the *Annals of Internal Medicine*, guys are bitten more often because, well, they're usually bigger, so there's more of them to bite. In addition, males emit more heat, exhale more carbon dioxide, and excrete more sweat, which is a volatile mixture of carbon dioxide, ammonia, lactic acid, and several carbolic acids. Skeeters love all this.

Pregnancy causes a woman's body to increase these same factors (more heat, more carbon dioxide, and more sweat). A pregnant woman attracts twice as many mosquitoes as a woman who is not pregnant.

Skeeters are simply sweeter on some of us.

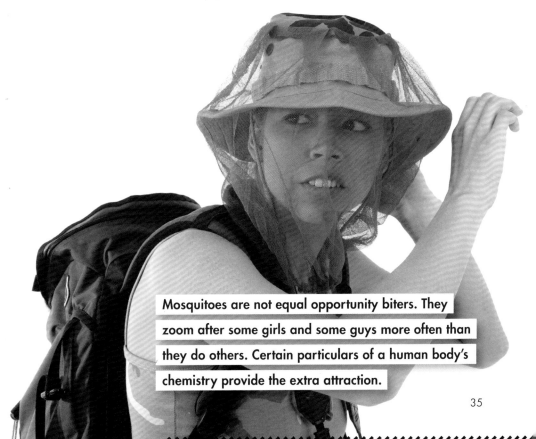

Mosquitoes are not equal opportunity biters. They zoom after some girls and some guys more often than they do others. Certain particulars of a human body's chemistry provide the extra attraction.

15 WEIGHT, WEIGHT DON'T TELL ME!

The more boys around, the more girls tend to change . . . what?

Girls seem to like changing things—outfits, screen savers, hair color—more than guys do. But why, when it comes to eating, do girls change what and how much they eat—not deliberately!—when guys are around?

A study of undergraduates at McMaster University in Ontario, Canada, showed that the more boys at a table, the fewer calories a girl consumes. Boys did not change their caloric intake whether one girl or a gaggle of gals joined the table.

Why do more guys mean girls eat less? Turns out girls, particularly between the ages of seventeen and twenty, believe boys are more attracted to females who eat less. Psychologist Meredith Young asserts that girls go low-cal because "salad leaves are meant to say, 'I'm pretty, I'm attractive, I take care of myself.'" Are girls justified in being so calorie conscious? The *International Journal of Obesity* reported that even a modest weight gain puts girls at risk of discrimination. Yet, society cuts guys much more slack when, well, they can't fit into their slacks.

Doctors use body mass index (BMI)—a relationship between height and weight—to measure a person's body fat. In general, a healthy BMI falls between 18.5 and 24.9. Weight-based harassment can begin for a girl whose BMI hits 27, roughly 13 pounds (5.9 kilograms) over her healthy weight. A guy's BMI can reach 35—68 pounds (30.8 kg) of extra weight—before he experiences similar discrimination.

So, are guys weight *unconscious*? Not according to *Psychology of Addictive Behaviors*. This journal published a study that says college guys are twice as likely to exercise to excess. And when these gym rats miss a scheduled workout, they are more likely to feel stress and irritability than are girls who miss a workout. When it comes to shedding pounds, scientific evidence suggests that, in general, girls count carbs and fats, while guys count laps and reps.

Now that's something to chew on!

Sharing meals together creates and maintains social bonds. But girls find a table that's gender mixed more loaded with social expectations.

16 WITHOUT A CLUE

Guys are so clueless. They can't even tell the difference between a polite smile and a flirty grin. True or false?

Sorry, guys. It's true.

Studies show that compared with teen girls, teen guys have more difficulty distinguishing between an impish smile that shows an interest in something more and an innocent smile that shows an interest in nothing more than smiling.

Researcher Coreen Farris at Indiana University's Department of Psychological and Brain Sciences recruited 280 undergrads of both sexes. They all viewed 280 women's faces and had to label them as (a) sexually interested, (b) friendly, (c) sad, or (d) rejected. Girls read the faces more accurately than guys. Males had two clear downfalls. They confused friendly with flirtatious faces, and they failed to sense the differences between a face showing sadness and a face expressing rejection.

It turns out that facial mimicry is a crucial part of empathy—responding to emotions in others.

Researchers have found that sucking on pacifiers takes away crucial time for babies to practice mimicry with those same facial muscles. This is particularly true for guys, who generally lag in emotional intelligence. College guys whose babyhood cries were stanched with a stopper—compared to those who were at liberty to burble, bubble, and bawl—performed less well on tests that involved assessing another individual's moods or expressions.

Why don't pacifiers pose such problems for girls? "Girls develop earlier," according to psychology professor Paula Niedenthal, "and it is possible that they make sufficient progress in emotional development before or despite pacifier use." Her research, published in *Basic and Applied Social Psychology*, suggests that boys may be more vulnerable to this disruption of mimicry. And because gender stereotyping portrays guys as more stoic, parents don't look for ways to support their sons' emotional intelligence.

So, girls, show some pity! Even if a guy might not recognize it.

Reading facial expressions is a key part of emotional intelligence. Both sexes need to interpret what another human is feeling and communicating. But pacifiers may be getting in the way of developing these skills for boy babies.

39

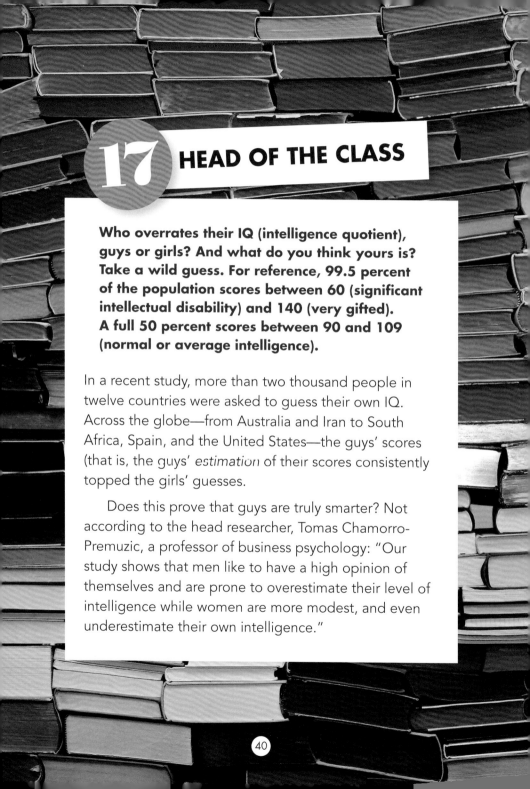

17 HEAD OF THE CLASS

Who overrates their IQ (intelligence quotient), guys or girls? And what do you think yours is? Take a wild guess. For reference, 99.5 percent of the population scores between 60 (significant intellectual disability) and 140 (very gifted). A full 50 percent scores between 90 and 109 (normal or average intelligence).

In a recent study, more than two thousand people in twelve countries were asked to guess their own IQ. Across the globe—from Australia and Iran to South Africa, Spain, and the United States—the guys' scores (that is, the guys' *estimation* of their scores consistently topped the girls' guesses.

Does this prove that guys are truly smarter? Not according to the head researcher, Tomas Chamorro-Premuzic, a professor of business psychology: "Our study shows that men like to have a high opinion of themselves and are prone to overestimate their level of intelligence while women are more modest, and even underestimate their own intelligence."

Curious to know in what parts of the world male egos are particularly inflated? In France, guys awarded themselves an extra fifteen points. The smallest difference between the sexes' estimates—only three points—occurred among Israelis and Iranians. The two other countries where guys think more highly of their intelligence? The United Kingdom and the United States, where guys' numbers were ten points higher than girls'. What's ten points? Enough to boost a score from average to superior intelligence.

Why such hubris, boys? Why such humility, girls? Chalk it up to societies around the world that prize assertiveness in men and modesty in women, the researchers suggest.

That smarts a bit, doesn't it?

The intelligence quotient, or IQ, is one way to rate or compare an individual's smarts. Consistently, in countries throughout the world, guys overrate their scores much more than girls do.

18 THE KEY(BOARD) TO HAPPINESS

Of all the things that can be done online, what's one thing that really captures a guy's attention?

More territory! More captives!

When guys play action video games, the gray matter lights up like a pinball machine. (Gray matter is the brain's neural cell bodies and dendrites involved in operations such as muscle control, sensory perception, memory, emotions, and speech.) When girls play—well, mostly, they don't play those types of video games.

Popular video games of aggression and territory feed into the brain's reward center. A pleasurable sensation—whether a delicious food, the comfort of petting a cat, or even the thought of doing something forbidden or risky—stimulates the brain's cerebral cortex to signal the neighboring ventral tegmental area to release a chemical called dopamine, which reaches the amygdala, prefrontal cortex, and nucleus accumbens. These three centers of the brain create the reward, a feeling of gratification. The brain says to itself, "Again!" and "Yes, more please!"

Dr. Allan Reiss's team of researchers at Stanford University hooked up male and female players to a magnetic resonance imaging (MRI) scanner. Both sexes competed in video games involving balls, scores, territories, and opponents. The more players a competitor vanquished and the more points he or she tallied, the more the brain's reward center fired up with activity.

Data from the gaming industry does show that more girls are becoming online gamers—almost 50 percent of all gamers are female. In fact, more women over eighteen (30 percent) are gaming than are boys under seventeen (17 percent). But females tend to opt out of games with shooting artillery and combat adventures in favor of games involving role playing, communication, and character creation. And these don't tap into the reward center of the female brain. Reiss concluded, "I think it's fair to say that males tend to be more [naturally] territorial. It doesn't take a genius to figure out who historically are the conquerors and tyrants of our species—they're the males."

Game over.

Girls and guys both enjoy gaming, but the thrills each sex is seeking comes from different types of games, which light up different parts of the brain.

19 SILENCE IS GOLDEN?

Some recent research alleges that girls, at the end of a day, tally thirteen thousand more of something than guys. What would that be? And is it really true?

In a word, the answer is words.

In her best-selling book *The Female Brain* (2006), Louann Brizendine claimed that women speak twenty thousand words in a day, while men utter only about seven thousand.

Well, that "fact" has been widely debunked through further studies involving larger populations and broader demographics. The most current information suggests that women knock out just over sixteen thousand words each day, while men utter something just shy of that. Statistically speaking, there is no significant difference.

So, why the lingering stereotype that ladies are chatty and guys are the strong, silent type? Psychologist Matthias Mehl of the University of Arizona at Tucson points out that the stereotype persists from centuries of women not working outside the home. In a typical scenario, the husband comes home from work. He's used up most of his daily quotient of words at the office. Maybe he's got 150 words left. He's ready to relax. But his spouse? She's still got her whole day's worth of words, and she's ready to serve them along with the nice hot dinner she's cooked.

But in the twenty-first century, women *outnumber* men in the US workforce. Are these workers winding down their day with another round of chatter? Not hardly.

Another discovery from Mehl's research team shows that women use more pronouns than men. Women talk more about relationships. On the other hand, men use more numbers. They talk more about sports and gadgets. A contemporary conversation might go something like this:

Woman: Did you hear that Mary broke up with him? And that she won't give him her new cell number?

Man: It's 7–4, bottom of the third, the number one team in the nation—Mary who?

Stereotypes say that girls talk more than guys. Science says no real data support this idea.

20 MAN OF MY DREAMS

Who dreams more about guys, males or females?

The news from snooze studies shows that males are 67 percent of the cast in men's dreams. But men are only 52 percent of the characters in women's dreams.

For most guys, their dreams focus on conflict scenarios, such as dealing with aggressors in strange places. And the aggressors are male.

Girls' dreams tend to be about encounters with family and friends in familiar places. The gender cast is about half male and half female. Or their dreams are romantic fantasies (though guys do dream more about sex than girls do).

Whatever the subject, girls recall their dreams more vividly and more frequently than guys. Psychology professor Jennifer Parker of the University of the West of England suggests that women take more of their day's concerns to bed, which leads to more emotionally intense dreams. In fact, girls consider 34 percent of their dreams to be nightmares, nearly twice as many as the 19 percent that men report as bad dreams.

Maybe the French poet Paul Valéry was right when he said, "The best way to make your dreams come true is to wake up."

The dream worlds of girls and guys don't have the same cast of characters—or the same plotlines either.

21 COOTIE OR CUTIE?

"Ewww, boys have cooties!" Does this age-old insult have any truth behind it? *Are* guys dirtier than girls?

According to a recent study, guys are indeed the grimier sex.

Researchers at South Dakota State University and at the University of Arizona swabbed the office chairs, desks, keyboards, and phones of both girls and guys in search of bacterial content. They found about one billion bacteria in every meter (3 feet) of office airspace.

Gross, huh? They also found about 10 to 20 percent more bacteria around the guys' chairs, desks, keyboards, and phones. The (founded? unfounded?) stereotype says that this is because boys have a more slovenly nature. That's a fancy way of saying that guys brush their teeth and wash their hands less often than girls. Well, that's true in both cases.

But before writing off guys as slobs, the researchers also proposed another possible cause.

Guys have less immaculate hygiene habits. But scientists believe that males may simply have more bacteria because—don't be shocked!—*they're bigger*. Bigger bodies equal more surface area for bacteria.

While boys definitely do have more cooties than girls, there's no need for alarm. Scientists say the amount of bacteria they found in the study is typical of a healthy, normal environment.

That means we can all get over this kookiness about cooties.

Bigger may not mean better in every case, but from a bacterium's point of view, a guy's larger body provides just that much more real estate.

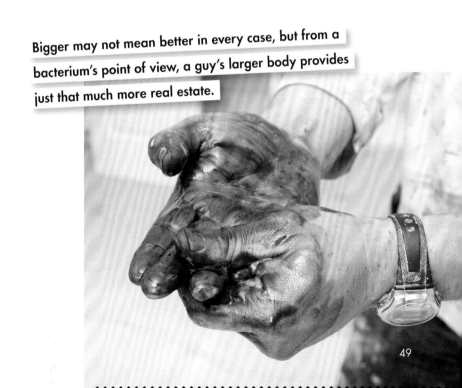

Maybe guys do this better in the dark, but girls do this better and faster overall. What is it?

Okay, guys, pound this into your brain. It takes a female less time than it does a male to hammer a nail into a board.

So, how long is that? Just long enough for the boys to rev up a witty remark: "As much time as it takes for her to bug me to do it for her!"

(One guy's grin is another girl's groan.)

Hammers are a pretty ancient tool. Humans have been wielding them for eons. So, why the difference between the sexes? Why, despite a guy's supposed handiness, DIY-ishness, and boastful expertise, have girls proven to be more accurate with a hammer?

As reported in *Scientific American*, researchers don't exactly know. They theorize that "maybe girls and boys inherently use different strategies, putting

more emphasis on either force or accuracy." What? Males and females do things differently? Ah, the wonders of research!

While guys hit the nail with twice as much force, girls are 25 percent more accurate no matter the target's size— that is, as long as there's adequate light. In *poor* lighting conditions, males are 10 percent more likely to hit the nail on the head. (In case you want to do the research yourself, dim the lights and put glow-in-the-dark stickers on the objects you want to hammer. Spooky!) Turns out "hitting the nail on the head" is not just a matter of pounding power or pinpointing targets.

So, gentlemen, if the lights are bright, pass the hammer.

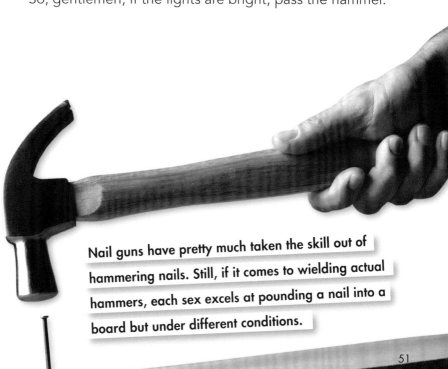

Nail guns have pretty much taken the skill out of hammering nails. Still, if it comes to wielding actual hammers, each sex excels at pounding a nail into a board but under different conditions.

23 DON'T SWEAT THE SMALL STUFF

Girls are made of "sugar and spice and all things nice." Boys are made of "slugs and snails and puppy dogs' tails." Then why does one sex smell of onions and the other of cheese?

You and your friends are sweating it out in a spin class. Swiss researchers join you in the locker room to analyze your underarm secretions. What do they discover—other than the fact that no one can resist jeering that their study stinks? Guys smell of cheese. Girls, of onion or grapefruit.

Christian Starkenmann, a flavor and fragrance scientist in Switzerland, discovered that women's armpits possess more of an odorless, sulfur-containing compound. Local skin bacteria ripen it into something that's got the reek of a leek. (Sweat by itself is actually odorless. What we smell is the product of bacteria feasting on sweat and body oils.)

A guy's sweat possesses more of a particular fatty acid. Bacteria give it an unmistakable cheesy odor.

But is sex the airbender here? Professor Tim Jacob of Cardiff University in the United Kingdom studies the psychophysiology of smell. He remains dubious. He suggests that "what you eat, what you wash with, what you wear, and what genes you inherit" together determine whether an individual's body odor gets an OK or a KO.

Even so, scent isn't the only difference between girls and guys. Girls and guys who haven't reached puberty have similar sweat rates. With the teen years and sexual maturity, hormones kick in and sweating patterns change. Testosterone (the male hormone) increases the amount and rate of sweating. In fact, guys injected with the female hormone estrogen sweat less.

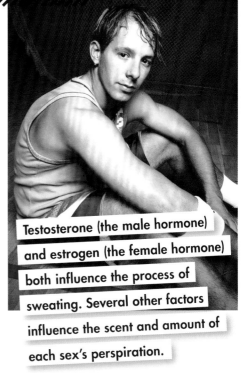

Testosterone (the male hormone) and estrogen (the female hormone) both influence the process of sweating. Several other factors influence the scent and amount of each sex's perspiration.

And get this. The fitter the person, the sweatier. People who are less fit can produce the same amount of sweat as their buff friends—but only at higher temperatures and with more work intensity. This is especially true for women.

Fit men perspire significantly more than fit women. In one study, Japanese researchers determined this wasn't because guys have more sweat glands. (They do.) Girls simply produce less sweat per gland. They are less biologically engineered to drench their skin to cool down, but the little perspiration they *do* create is more efficient at thermoregulation.

You might say boys are built for heat. And girls are made for the shade.

24 MIRROR, MIRROR ON THE WALL . . .

When it comes to Facebook, who's vainer? Girls or guys?

Surprisingly, or not surprisingly (depending on what you guessed), guys are.

Women are often considered the vainer sex. And readers often misquote Shakespeare's line from *Hamlet*, "Frailty, thy name is woman," as "Vanity, thy name is woman." Yet, more and more evidence points to guys as the vain sex.

Of Gen-Y kids (those born in the 1980s, the 1990s, and the early 2000s), 25 percent of the guys doctor their Facebook pics to look more flattering, while 14 percent of girls do. And when it comes to selfies, 17 percent of guys shoot and post pics of themselves, while only 10 percent of women do.

Of course, evidence of vanity can be gathered from a host of contexts and behaviors. For instance, the US Bureau of Labor Statistics conducts its American Time Use Survey each year. While girls

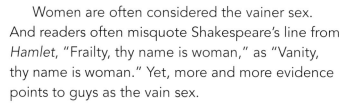

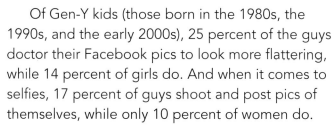

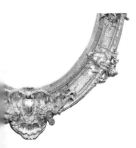

spend more time showering, drying their hair, and applying products to their faces, guys have been steadily adding minutes to their grooming routines for the last ten years or so. They've gone from thirty-seven minutes each day to more than forty-five minutes. Girls spend around fifty-four minutes each day, dropping a couple minutes in the last few years.

About 70 percent of American men between the ages of eighteen and twenty-four now scruff or buff or squirt their faces before they head out. According to consumer-trends tracker Mintel, launches of new personal-care products for men increased globally by 70 percent between 2007 and 2012.

So, who's gazing in the reflection, wondering who's the fairest of them all? Increasingly, there's a man in the mirror.

On average, girls spend more time fussing with their looks in front of a mirror than guys do. But studies show that males are more obsessed with how they look in photos.

25 OUT OF YOUR LEAGUE

A (straight) guy is doing a Sudoku puzzle in a room with an attractive man and an attractive woman. The attractive man leaves the room. Five minutes later, what's going on inside the head of the guy who's doing the puzzle?

His cortisol is spiking.

The adrenal glands produce cortisol when the body is stressed—physically or mentally. In modest measures, it increases alertness and offers a sense of well-being. But higher or chronic levels increase blood pressure, sexual dysfunction, and a host of other less desirable things. So, what's the stress of being left alone with a beautiful woman? It triggers the possibility of courting . . . and that makes a (straight) guy anxious. The adrenal glands pump out more cortisol.

In one study, researchers used the subjects' saliva to test for the amount of cortisol. When a guy viewed a woman as particularly attractive—out of his league, even—the cortisol level in his saliva increased even more. (Nope, this isn't where the expression "drooling over" comes from.)

In this same study, when the attractive woman left the room, the presence of the handsome man in the room didn't cause a rise in the cortisol for the guy working the Sudoku game.

Wonder what the results would be with gay and lesbian subjects? Would their cortisol rise after five minutes in the presence of an attractive member of the same sex?

Still to be studied.

The human body releases certain chemicals in reaction to physical and mental stress. A recent study shows that—at least for guys— beauty can be one of those stress factors.

26 WHAT'S ON YOUR MIND, GUYS?

Girls do this once a day. Guys . . . something like every fifty-two seconds. And what would that be?

Check their cell phones? Flex a bicep in front of a reflective surface? Scan the local environment for something to scarf down? Good guesses, but that's not it.

With 86,400 seconds in a day, most people use about one-third of those seconds sleeping. That leaves almost 58,000 waking seconds for thinking about everything else that makes your world go round. That's everything from remembering to turn on your alarm to clicking off pop-up ads, hovering over the bagel in the toaster, ignoring the whines of siblings, finding your keys, watching, writing, daydreaming, worrying over—*whoosh*.

And, if you're a guy, 1,108 sexual thoughts—that's one every fifty-two seconds—flash through your mind during a typical day. Meanwhile, if you're a girl, your brain has entertained 1,107 fewer sexual thoughts. (Let's do the math: 1,108 − 1,107 = 1 sexual thought.)

This incredible imbalance has plenty of supporters *and* plenty of doubters. But even the most conservative points of view will grant that guys are more preoccupied with sex than girls. This is due, in part, because they have 2.5 times more brain space focused on sex—particularly, a bigger amygdala. This mass of gray matter in each brain hemisphere is devoted to fear, aggression, visual learning, and memory. In zoological and evolutionary terms, male mammals use these skills to compete for females. So, it's their task to hint at the topic of, you know, making babies, while women spend their 1,107 nonsexual thoughts on other vital topics.

True enough: guys *do* have sex on the brain.

By counting thoughts, researchers have found that men do indeed think more about sex than women do.

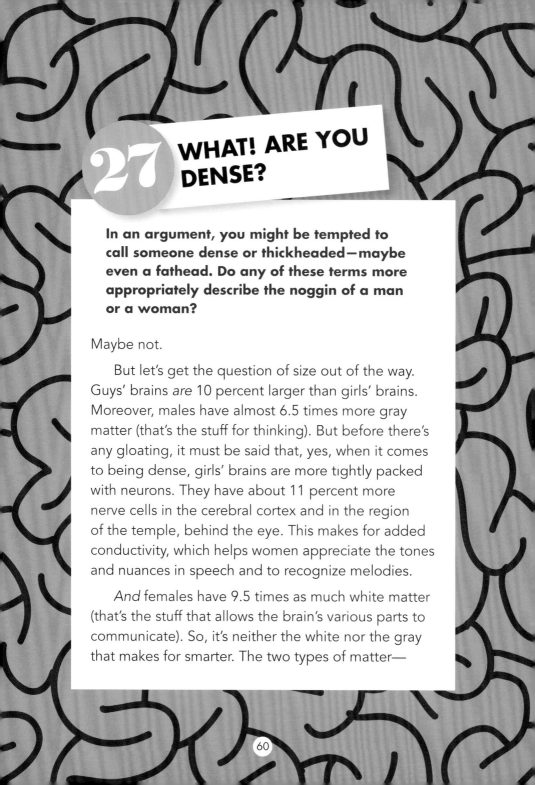

27 WHAT! ARE YOU DENSE?

In an argument, you might be tempted to call someone dense or thickheaded—maybe even a fathead. Do any of these terms more appropriately describe the noggin of a man or a woman?

Maybe not.

But let's get the question of size out of the way. Guys' brains *are* 10 percent larger than girls' brains. Moreover, males have almost 6.5 times more gray matter (that's the stuff for thinking). But before there's any gloating, it must be said that, yes, when it comes to being dense, girls' brains are more tightly packed with neurons. They have about 11 percent more nerve cells in the cerebral cortex and in the region of the temple, behind the eye. This makes for added conductivity, which helps women appreciate the tones and nuances in speech and to recognize melodies.

And females have 9.5 times as much white matter (that's the stuff that allows the brain's various parts to communicate). So, it's neither the white nor the gray that makes for smarter. The two types of matter—

and the density of the matter—make for different sorts of smarts.

Girls *are* the thicker-headed sex. The thickness of their skulls averages 7.1 millimeters (0.28 inches) compared to 6.5 millimeters (0.26 in.) for guys. And, yes, that 0.6 millimeter (0.02 in.) difference provides just that much more protection for all that *matters* inside.

Ford Motor Company commissioned this comparative study, which the *International Journal of Vehicle Safety* published. (Yes, there's a journal that covers subjects you never even thought to worry your head about.) The intention was to help in the design and manufacture of safety devices for preventing head injury in collisions. The study of three thousand people also revealed that front-to-back skull measurements averaged 176 millimeters (6.9 in.) for men and 171 millimeters (6.7 in.) for women. And skull width? Men averaged 145 millimeters (5.7 in.), and women averaged 140 millimeters (5.5 in.). This isn't a lot of hard data to go on, but researchers speculate that skull shape and thickness both contribute to survival.

So, if someone calls you thickheaded, you can point them to the science to prove it's, well, a compliment.

Male and female skulls have detectable, although subtle, differences that become more distinct after puberty. For instance, guys have more blocklike foreheads with a more pronounced browridge over the eyes. Girls have less prominent cheekbones and pointier lower jaws.

28 I WISH I . . .

A genie offers you three wishes on one condition: a wish can be used only for changing your physical appearance. Does the genie hear the same requests from both girls and guys?

Sort of.

In 2012 InSites Consulting conducted a sixteen-country survey of 4,065 kids between the ages of fifteen and twenty-five. The company discovered that 88 percent of the females would opt for a little magical transformation of the body, specifically the stomach, bottom, thighs, and breasts.

And the males? When it comes to abs, muscles, chests, mouths, and cheeks, 73 percent of boys would cue up for some presto chango.

Lead researcher and author of *How Cool Brands Stay Hot*, Joeri Van den Bergh points out that experts in many fields frequently consider the current generation of youth "as the most narcissistic group ever." Talk about immodesty, 69 percent of the US kids surveyed claimed to be "unique." (How can seven out of ten all be unique?) Some even considered themselves "very unique." (For those of us who wish to preserve the meaning of the word *unique*—exclusive, one of a kind— that's like awarding two first prizes.)

Only 7 percent of the participating kids were willing to dismiss the genie's offer altogether. This small subset of the study was content. Among the American kids, 21 percent of the guys were proud of their whole body, with eyes (34 percent), hair (22 percent), and skin (14 percent) ranking highest among body parts. Only 7 percent of US girls in the study were happy with their whole body, with eyes (48 percent), hair (36 percent), and chests (18 percent) garnering the most pride.

So, what's the one-and-only wish both sexes might consider asking of the genie? "Please, make me content with my body."

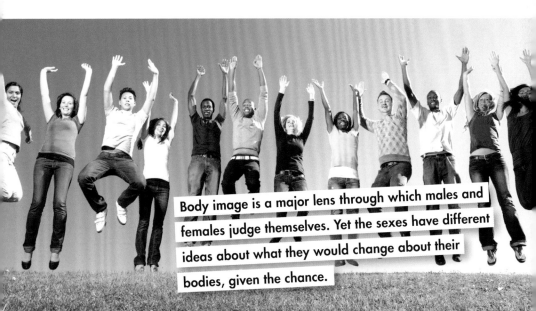

Body image is a major lens through which males and females judge themselves. Yet the sexes have different ideas about what they would change about their bodies, given the chance.

WRAPPING IT UP

So, after passing through some of the charted—and uncharted—waters that divide the sexes, you might ask yourself, "What kinds of general conclusions do researchers come to about men and women?"

"Although gender differences, on average, are not under dispute, the idea of consistently and inflexibly gender-typed individuals is," writes Bobbi J. Carothers of Washington University and Harry T. Reis of the University of Rochester. In thirteen studies, they assessed 122 characteristics in 13,301 guys and girls. Their conclusion? "There are not two distinct genders, but instead, there are linear gradations of variables associated with sex, such as masculinity or intimacy, all of which are continuous."

Increasingly, science can unlock these age-old yet ever-evolving mysteries. As neuroscientist Dr. Bennett A. Shaywitz, chief of pediatric neurology at the Yale University School of Medicine, points out, "It is a truism that men and women are different. What . . . we can do now is to take what is essentially folklore and place it in the context of science. There is a real scientific method available to answer some of these questions [about the sexes]."

Got it, guys? Got it, girls? Maybe instead of imagining that murky waters divide the sexes, try thinking that we're all in the pool together. We all swim at our own risk. We're all in over our heads. And in real life, no guards are on duty. And that's why we need the buddy system. It works.

To sum it all up, the one thing to keep in mind that can make a world of difference in understanding guys and girls is to remember that a range of variables inform male and female identities.

The Human Brain

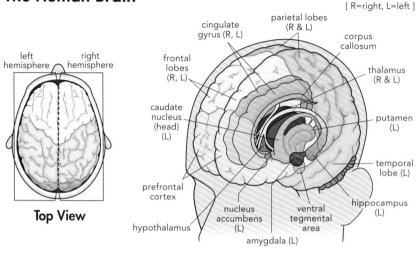

left hemisphere

right hemisphere

Top View

cingulate gyrus (R, L)

parietal lobes (R & L)

corpus callosum

frontal lobes (R, L)

thalamus (R & L)

caudate nucleus (head) (L)

putamen (L)

temporal lobe (L)

prefrontal cortex

hippocampus (L)

nucleus accumbens (L)

ventral tegmental area

hypothalamus

amygdala (L)

corpus callosum

cingulate gyrus

frontal lobe

caudate nucleus (head)

parietal lobe

prefrontal cortex

occipital lobe

temporal lobe

amygdala

nucleus accumbens

putamen

ventral tegmental area

Cross Section, Right Hemisphere

Cerebral Cortex

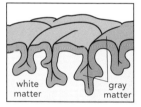

white matter

gray matter

The cerebral cortex is the outermost layer of the brain, consisting of gray matter (neural cell bodies) and white matter (nerve fibers that communicate information).

SOURCE NOTES

16   David K. Dodd, "Smiling in School Yearbook Photos: Gender Differences from Kindergarten to Adulthood." *Psychological Record* 49 (1999): 543–554.

17   Ibid.

17   Ibid.

17   Ibid.

18   Colin Lecher, "FYI: Why Do Girls Throw Like a Girl?" *Popular Science*, September 18, 2012, accessed January 9, 2014, http://www.popsci.com /science/article/2012-09/fyi-do-men-and-women-throw-ball-differently.

18–19 Tamar Haspel, "Throw Like a Girl? You Can Do Better," *Washington Post*, September 10, 2012, accessed January 9, 2014, http://www .washingtonpost.com/national/health-science/throw-like-a-girl-with -some-practice-you-can-do-better/2012/09/10/9ffc8bc8-dc09-11e1 -9974-5c975ae4810f_story.html.

19   Lecher, "FYI."

21   Richard Alleyne, "Women's Voices 'Make Plants Grow Faster' Finds Royal Horticultural Society," *Telegraph*, (London), June 22, 2009, accessed January 6, 2014, http://www.telegraph.co.uk/earth /earthnews/5602419/Womens-voices-make-plants-grow-faster-finds -Royal-Horticultural-Society.html.

36   Aditya Chkrabortty, "Brain Food: Why Women Eat Salad, *Guardian*, (Manchester), February 1, 2010, accessed January 6, 2014, http://www .guardian.co.uk/science/2010/feb/02/brain-food-why-women-eat-salad.

39   University of Wisconsin–Madison, "Pacifiers May Have Emotional Consequences for Boys," *ScienceDaily*, September 12, 2012, accessed January 6, 2014, http://www.sciencedaily.com /releases/2012/09/120918154112.htm?utm_source=feedburner&utm _medium=feed&utm_campaign=Feed%3A+sciencedaily+%28Science Daily%3A+Latest+Science+News%29.

40   "International Men of Immodesty," *Medical News Today*, April 20, 2009, accessed January 6, 2014, http://www.medicalnewstoday.com /releases/146698.php.

43   Michelle L. Brandt, "Video Games Activate Reward Regions of Brain in Men More Than Women, Stanford Study Says," *Standford School of Medicine*, February 4, 2008, accessed January 6, 2014, http://med .stanford.edu/news_releases/2008/february/videobrain.html.

47   "Paul Valéry Quotes," *Brainy Quote*, 2014, accessed January 6, 2014, http://www.brainyquote.com/quotes/authors/p/paul_valery.html.

50–51 Christie Nicholson, "Women Better Than Men with a Hammer," *Scientific American*, June 30, 2009, accessed January 6, 2014, http://www.scientificamerican.com/podcast/episode.cfm?id=women-better-than-men-with-a-hammer-09-06-30.

52   Elisabeth Knowles, ed., *Oxford Dictionary of Quotations*, 5th ed. (New York: Oxford University Press, 1999), 551.

52   Gretchen Reynolds, "Phys Ed: Do Women Sweat Differently Than Men?" *New York Times*, October 20, 2010, accessed January 6, 2014, http://well.blogs.nytimes.com/2010/10/20/do-women-sweat-differently-than-men.

54   William Shakespeare, "No Fear Shakespeare, Hamlet: Act 1, Sciene 2, Page 6," *Spark Notes*, accessed January 7, 2014, http://nfs.sparknotes.com/hamlet/page_28.html.

62   Joeri Van den Jergh, "Fifteen Percent of US Youngsters Consider Plastic Surgery," *InSites Consulting*, June 26, 2012, accessed January 7, 2014, http://www.insites-consulting.com/press/15-of-us-youngsters-consider-plastic-surgery.

64   Eric W. Dolan, "Study Debunks Notion That Men and Women Are Psychologically Distinct," *Raw Story*, February 4, 2013, accessed January 6, 2014, http://www.rawstory.com/rs/2013/02/04/study-debunks-notion-that-men-and-women-are-psychologically-distinct.

64   Ibid.

64   Gina Kolata, "Man's World, Woman's World? Brain Studies Point to Differences," *New York Times*, February 28, 1995, accessed February 7, 2014, http://www.nytimes.com/1995/02/28/science/man-s-world-woman-s-world-brain-studies-point-to-differences.html.

SELECTED BIBLIOGRAPHY

Baron-Cohen, Simon. *The Essential Difference: Men, Women and the Extreme Male Brain*. London: Penguin, 2012.

Elliot, Lise. *Pink Brain, Blue Brain*. Boston: Houghton Mifflin Harcourt, 2009.

Fine, Cordelia. *Delusions of Gender: How Our Minds, Society, and Neurosexism Create Difference*. New York: Norton, 2010.

Gray, John. *Men Are from Mars, Women Are from Venus*. New York: HarperCollins, 1993.

Hines, Elissa. *Brain Gender*. New York: Oxford University Press, 2004.

Hyde, Jane Shibley. "The Gender Similarities Hypothesis." *American Psychologist*, 581–592, 60, no. 6 (2005). http://www.careerpioneernetwork .org/wwwroot/userfiles/files/the_gender_similarities_hypothesis.pdf.

Moir, Anne, and Bill Moir. *Why Men Don't Iron: The Science of Gender Studies*. New York: Citadel, 2000.

PsychCentral, 2014. Accessed January 15, 2014. http://psychcentral.com.

"Search Archives: Men Women." *ScienceDaily*. 2014. Accessed January 27. 2014. http://www.sciencedaily.net/search/?keyword=men+women.

"Search Results: Men and Women." *Live Science.com*. 2014. Accessed January 15, 2014. http://www.livescience.com/search.html?cx=partner-pub -1894578950532504%3Aqaei7k190hq&cof=FORID%3A10&ie=ISO-8859- 1&sa=&q=men+women.

"Social Sciences News." Phys.org, 2014. Accessed January 27, 2014. http:// phys.org/science-news/social-sciences.

"Well Blog: Men Women Search Results." *New York Times*. 2014. Accessed February 1, 2014. http://well.blogs.nytimes.com/?s=men+women.

FOR FURTHER INFORMATION

Books

Brynie, Faith Hickman. *101 Questions about Sex and Sexuality . . . with Answers for the Curious, Cautious, and Confused*. Minneapolis: Twenty-First Century Books, 2003.

———. *101 Questions Your Brain Has Asked about Itself but Couldn't Answer . . . Until Now*. Minneapolis: Twenty-First Century Books, 2007.

Eastham, Chal. *Guys Are Waffles, Girls Are Spaghetti*. Nashville: Thomas Nelson, 2009.

Hanan, Jessica. *Coping with Changing Roles for Young Men and Women*. New York: Rosen, 2000.

Pease, Allan, and Barbara Pease. *Why Men Don't Listen and Why Women Can't Read Maps*. New York: Broadway Books, 2001.

Pfaff, Donald W. *Man and Woman: An Inside Story*. New York: Oxford University Press, 2010.

Wilson, Michael R. *Frequently Asked Questions about How the Teen Brain Works*. New York: Rosen, 2010.

Winston, Robert. *What Makes Me, Me?* New York: DK Children, 2004.

Websites

New York Times
http://www.query.nytimes.com/search/sitesearch/#/difference+men+women
The *New York Times* online archives offer many well-written feature stories and briefs by experts or journalists on topics related to gender differences.

Phys.org
http://www.phys.org
A vast and comprehensive science and technology site, Phys.org aggregates five hundred articles each week from a variety of reputable sources. Subjects include biology, social sciences, physics, and medicine. Using "sex" and "difference" as search tags produces a rich variety of articles on the science of gender differences.

Psychology Today
http://www.psychologytoday.com
The online publication home of *Psychology Today* magazine engages hundreds of psychiatrists, authors, and professors to write on everything related to the mind. The site also features a vast range of self-assessments—quizzes to test everything from anxiety level to mental speed and flirtation to hostility. (Basic score and results are free. Full reports cost money.)

Science News
http://www.sciencenewsforkids.org
The online publication of the Society for Science and the Public features articles on a wide range of subjects. Search their archives under the headings of "Body & Health" and "Brain & Behavior" for articles related to this book.

TeensHealth.org
http://www.teenshealth.org
Operated by the nonprofit Nemours Center for Children's Health Media, this site provides accurate, accessible information for teens on topics relating to emotions, health, and healthy living.

INDEX

PHOTO ACKNOWLEDGMENTS

The images in this book are used with the permission of: © Iscatel/Shutterstock.com, p.1 (letter *U*); © Serg64/Shutterstock.com, p. 1 (letter *L*); © aastock/Shutterstock.com, p. 1, (bottom *G*); © photokup/Shutterstock.com, p. 1, (top *G*); © DeSerg/Shutterstock.com, p. 1, (top *S*); © Daniel Hjalmarson/Shutterstock.com, p. 1, 14 (letter *R*); © Keith Lamond /Shutterstock.com, p. 1, (bottom *S*); © Elenadesigns/Shutterstock.com, p. 1, (letter *I*); © iStockphoto.com/Henrik5000, p. 1, (letter *Y*); © Jose Marques/Shutterstock.com, p. 3; © Derter/Shutterstock.com, p. 6, 7; © Juan He/Shutterstock.com, p. 8; © Ace Stock Limited/Alamy, p. 9; © Tronin Andrei/Shutterstock.com, p. 10; © Jupiterimages/Photos .com/Thinkstock, p. 11; © UpperCut Images/Alamy, p. 12; © Laurence Mouton/PhotoAlto /Getty Images, p. 13; © Wavebreak Media/Thinkstock, p. 15; © iko/Shutterstock .com, p. 16 © nensuria/iStock/Thinkstock, p. 17; © SixApril/Shutterstock.com, p. 18; © tr3gin/Shutterstock.com, p. 20; © Keith Lamond/Shutterstock.com, p. 22; © Marin Tomas/iStock/Thinkstock, p. 23; © rvvlada/Shutterstock.com, p. 24; © Petrenko Andriy /Shutterstock.com, p. 25; © STILLFX/Shutterstock.com, p. 26; © AVAVA/Shutterstock.com, p. 27; © olly/Shutterstock.com, p. 28; © Fuse/Thinkstock, p. 29; © Johanna Goodyear /Shutterstock.com, p. 30; © iStockphoto.com/Aratehortua , p. 32; © Rudyanto Wijaya /iStock/Thinkstock, p. 33; © Henrik Larsson/Shutterstock.com, p. 34; © Simone van den Berg/iStock/Thinkstock, p. 35; © Amero/Shutterstock.com, p. 36; © LuckyBusiness /iStock/Thinkstock, p. 37; © Ivan Masic/iStock/Thinkstock, p. 38; © Anne-Louise Quarfoth /iStock/Thinkstock, p. 39; © r.martens/Shutterstock.com, p. 40; © iStockphoto.com /kinnerean, p. 42; © iStockphoto.com/ranplett, p. 43; © iStockphoto.com/ulimi, p. 44; © Vadim Georgiev/Shutterstock.com, p. 46; © Adrin Shamsudin/iStock/Thinkstock, p. 47; © Fedorov Oleksiy/Shutterstock.com, p. 48; © iStockphoto.com/BanksPhotos, p. 49; © Thirteen/Shutterstock.com, p. 50; © Jupiterimages/Goodshoot/Thinkstock, p. 51; © iStockphoto.com/Macpherson Photo, p. 52; © Kati Neudert/iStock/Thinkstock, p. 53; © gillmar/Shutterstock.com, p. 54; © iStockphoto.com/Moncherie, p. 55; © iStockphoto .com/ilbusca, p. 56; © Anna Bizoa/iStock/Thinkstock, p. 57; © iStockphoto.com/Warchi, p. 58; © Madartists/Dreamstime.com, p. 59; © dimair/Shutterstock.com, p. 60; © Carlos Amarillo/Shutterstock.com, p. 62; © Christopher Futcher/iStock/Thinkstock, p. 63; © incredible_movement/Shutterstock.com, p. 64, 65; © Laura Westlund/Independent Picture Service, p. 66.

Front Cover: © Iscatel/Shutterstock.com, (letter *U*); © Serg64/Shutterstock.com, (letter *L*); © aastock/Shutterstock.com, (bottom *G*); © photokup/Shutterstock.com, (top *G*); © DeSerg/Shutterstock.com, (top *S*); © Daniel Hjalmarson/Shutterstock.com, (letter *R*); © Keith Lamond/Shutterstock.com, (bottom *S*); © Elenadesigns/Shutterstock.com, (letter *I*); © iStockphoto.com/Henrik5000, (letter *Y*).

ABOUT THE AUTHOR

Michael J. Rosen is the author of more than one hundred books for readers of all ages, including nonfiction, humor, poetry, young adult novels, anthologies, and picture books. He lives in the foothills of the Appalachians in Central Ohio. His website is www.fidosopher.com.